Disclaimer

Stories, names, characters, and incidents portrayed in this book are reflections of the author's recollected experiences over time. No identifications with actual persons (living or deceased), specific places and products are intended or should be inferred. Portrayals have been creatively changed in terms of compression and semi-fiction with a view to resonating with the emotional energy of focus. If in any mood distress, please contact relevant professionals.

Foreword

Reflecting writing, particularly freestyle and/or creative writing helped me become aware of and simply be with feelings (pleasant and unpleasant), a solace from unstoppable cognitive repeats. Here's to share a piece of work in the free spirit that when these emotions touch you, something positive, warm and creative flows your way to inspire you in your own journey of awareness and reflections, bringing you closer to you, just as you are.

Contents

#25 Powerless to Aware

Flashing light then yellow spots all around

My head feels light, I'm dizzy, going round

My stomach is tight, wait I'm sick

I cough and gag, spitting out brick

I'm feeling the heat, sweating profusely

Unable to pace myself and breathe freely

Then I hear fuss around me, loud and clear

Noises that bubble away in the distance along with my fear

All is quiet, cool, serene and dark

I can no longer remember that I'm a shark

I find myself swimming incessantly next time I open my eyes

Looking around, my fins are wrinkled and wise

I've been swimming forever, faster than I wish

I don't know my exact age but that I am an old fish

Yet I proudly look at my shining rich green-blue tail

And swim harder to find my bearings without fail

I swim towards shimmering blotches of yellow and white

A glimmer of hope, tiny windows with dimming light

On what seems to be a strong built, tall blue brick wall

With many windows and green creepers that fall

Not caring much for which door to take, I follow the current

Perhaps naive but these options feel no different

Thinking each window would probably lead to a similar view

I choose the second door and swim through

When on the other side I look back to spell

"Well" - I'm in between the wall around a well

Just as I realise I get sucked into the drain

And go spiralling down faster and further in vain

I then land on my feet, do I have ten toes down?

My spirits feel damp, I can no longer swim to not drown

#24 Insecurity to Insight

I am at the bottom of the well, for sure

Whether a fish, human or spirit obscure

Sudden drop in temperature makes me gasp for air

I hear loud bubbles and feel warm glare

I am sinking downwards and hit the floor

That jolts me to wake up on the other side of the shore

A sense of relief despite all the coughing

I am by the river with six younger siblings

And a mum, overworked as dad is absent

I emerge out of the waters saving a sibling at present

It's good to see my sibling safe yet I feel like a fool

As mother has decided to remove me from school

Above all, I value freedom and education the most

I work hard at home looking after kids like dad almost

I do feel for my mother who fights for us all

Even when she forces us to overeat amidst brawl

She is often agitated saying her life is unfair

But does that give her the right to despair?

Seeing my sisters get beaten has become a chore

Memories imprinted on all our spirits, forever sore

As I endeavour to stand, I fall back in the river

I see glimpses of my married life in a quiver

My wife often physically throws things my way

Unable to channel her passions and word play

I feel love for my mother, my wife and son

The latter has chosen to join the army and gun

He's my most cherished yet furthest away

All his life memories are forever with me to stay

I wonder what good came out of all my love

I gave and gave, happy or sad, push or shove

#23 Guilt to Action

I get rushedly swept away by the river swirl

And back to the bottom of the well pearl

I look up to the windows and hastily choose the first

Swimming through, I encounter waters more than thirst

Next I wake up as a young woman who's a gifted artist

Who pushes self closer to goals, posing a strong fist

I work and work, above anything, work is dear

With no people around, I have none to fear

Sometimes, only sometimes, I miss my partner who has left

How could he, after I put up with all his theft

I gather it's all up to me what I make of my life

It wasn't too bad when mum tossed a strife

I was only 9 then, I did cry truck loads

Suddenly I had to get along with dad and the toads

I had music that stayed a good friend

People are lovely until, until I offend

I know so much, I think and feel deep

So much so, it affects my eating and sleep

I'm chuffed with my art and music creations

All is fine until I fall for distractions

As the voice in my head goes louder still

Calling me useless, I grab a drink and a pill

There's a flood of tears and damp feelings

Self-medication becomes a plaster, my own healing

I want to feel, live better and for longer though

Could do with skipping days where I don't show

Yet I could have fallen and faded in between

And here I'm an artist like I dreamed at 13

My face knocks over my drink, I'm gone again

There is no respite until I find refrain

#22 Jealousy to Affirmation

Adamant to find a new solution, I swim across

Only to see many more windows covered in moss

Swimming through to a blind chance yet again

Here I am a school boy drenching in rain

I seriously don't know what's wrong with me

I just don't get it, I will never get a degree

This is what my parents and tutors say

And that I will fail all my exams anyway

They compare me to my brother when they can

Calling me names, for sure, they are not a fan

There is a loud, definite voice inside my head

It also says I will fail before I attempt instead

I have faced a lot of odds moving to a new country

Sensing a different palate, adjusting to the pantry

Helping my younger brother with his English

And my parents with paperwork without relinquish

I feel I have no one to speak to really

At least friends this year don't call me silly

Then a kind lady questions me if I feel pride and joy

In owning my role to help my brother, little boy

I guess I had never thought that way before

She then questions what I'd rather explore

I said I danced and helped as a school councillor

She shared how I brightened and looked fuller

I still did not know how to fix this voice inside

That's when she invited me to affirm "I'm good besides"

I simply mocked, "What good would that do?"

Yet within that week my confidence grew

I stepped out in the heavy rain once again

This time in delight, leaving behind the pain

#21 Hatred to Expansion

Back at the well, I look at the third

If only there was a clue or a word

I take a deep sigh and swim through it, but then

Get washed through a tunnel and out by the Fen

I see a tall chap with glasses, greeting another

The other looks a bit like his brother

They say something, then turn over to me

At this point, I have nowhere to hide or flee

I take up the offer, I will prove to them

Knowing little, amidst unduly condemn

As I strut around and judge in a huff

Underneath it all, I don't feel good enough

I need a change, a break to create some art

My head doesn't give way to my heart

I'm done smelling fumes of ethanol all day

I'd like my white robe to go on display

Nothing artistic here, I've been a weary chemist

Do I discover, or simply mass-produce by the list?

I scored triple A's to show the wide world

No more, at the expense of me hurled

So many rules, so many games

For status, finance, impact and fame

What about old-fashioned peace of mind?

A helping lifestyle, empathic and kind

My bank statements do not agree

I have responsibilities, I am not free

As I jump back in the Fen for a swim

I hear rock music mashed up with a hymn

I follow the dazzling light beneath

I find myself near Hampstead Heath

#20 Rage to Reality

I can feel the waters of the unexpected heavy rainfall

As I thought I was strolling on a perfect sunny day to a mall

I feel furious, I want to shout out and scream

I cannot believe my life is nothing like a dream

I don't fully feel like myself, I am exhausted

Exhausted of dealing with my wife's stead

She is so altogether, so organised in her head

I hate it, I feel all over the place instead

Why is she with me, so she can feel superior?

Or am I her personal piece of charity for an inferior?

When I take a break from her, I feel so much lighter

It doesn't last much though, I can sense my fighter

I then crave for chocolates, coffee and sport

Isn't that life, enjoying the pleasure you can afford?

Even then I feel a certain void in my heart

Someone is to blame for not fully playing their part

Perhaps it was my mother, who was unfit

Or my father who rarely saw me and when he did, he hit

Well that was the past, I am certain it is my wife

She is the sole reason to ruin my life

I know this because my heart fluttered again

As I met and got to know this amazing person, not in pain

She had cracked happiness, she didn't give a toss

She was into adventures like me, a rolling stone gathers no moss

Until she told me she had a husband and another partner

And a third one who had recently stopped speaking to her

I felt a bit confused but found solace in pretend

What has it got to do with me anyway, I am just a friend

Then she wanted more from me, what a mess

I'd like to be back in that heavy rainfall, I must confess

#19 Anger to Sensation

I find myself in a different river, it's burning and all engulfing

Like a giant, hissing serpent from out of nowhere, divulging

I know it is negative, can be evil, yet I cannot shake it off

The harder I push it down, it unexpectedly overspills as scoff

I am angry for trying so hard, fighting for what's right

Sometimes I am simply angry that I stand by the fight

I am angry no one seems to care just as much as I do

I am angry that I get judged when I am angry too

I am angry for all the longing to feel acknowledged

I am angry for feeling numb, working so hard in College

I am angry to be with a partner, clueless as to what to say

All he says is "You OK", "I had a good day" and "Hey"

He cannot see the hurt he's caused when he broke my trust

He cannot see I'm overwhelmed versus his quench for lust

I am angry to identify what's really not working

I am angry to make an effort at various forking

I am angry to not receive when overpromised

I wish I was devoid of responsibilities, I'd be pissed

I am angry to know all this and still feel stuck

I am angry to hit repeat, fight, numb and duck

I want to explore my anger, it takes a lot of energy

When turned in, it drains me and causes lethargy

I decide to write and use this energy as a fuel

Sometimes I simply voice my feelings, a raw duel

I acknowledge anger but I value compassion

Can this wild serpent be tamed in an orderly fashion?

Feeling the heat, I can sense the intense pain

A headless monster, running endlessly in vain

I decide to simply let the waters flow

In the hope of cooling this hurting fellow

#18 Disappointment to Dutiful

I'm swimming as I do, going through the motions

This is no fairy tale, there is no hero, no love potions

It's me sighing and deeply hurt, trekking up the island hill

The sun is scorching hot, and the air feels dead still

I have loved and trusted to be stabbed in my back

And it feels worse than swimming against the rocks' hack

Apparently I am the problem, sensitive and jealous

While he is the one honest, about texting endless

This should not be a problem, she is married

Plus has a long term partner with kids, also married

He insists he is doing no wrong, he will maintain friendship

Yet says nothing to her about her wanting a relationship

He says he is not looking at her when she poses half naked

Maybe he thinks I am compromised and completely wasted?

Apparently her texting at all times is justified as her husband is fine

Besides she has ADHD, and he might have it too, it's his moment to shine

Who am I to judge, each to their own, however where do I stand?

Am I simply waiting for the worst to happen and still understand?

I breathe and say to myself, ride with the waves and the wind

I cannot control the storm, the moonlight and their effects twinned

I am in power of how I feel and what I would like in my life

Would he have put up with all this if he were my wife?

I am not too sure because he cannot even tolerate

My anger for less than a minute, as I face my own ill fate

I realise I am not in an equal relationship of give and take

I give, feel exhausted and don't feel valued for my own sake

I don't know how to get out of this swimming cycle

If I left him, would I attract a similar yet unique Michael?

I swim and swim, fulfilling my duties, facing twists and turns

Not in vain, I am becoming aware of my relationships patterns

#17 Doubt to OK

Swimming is so healthy, how do I even feel anxiety?

Perhaps I have done enough, time to pause for a cuppa of herbal tea

As I swim to the water kettle, It can't be that simple, says logic

Yet something else answers, But often at its simplest hides magic

Isn't it understandable that anyone can feel overwhelmed

When juggling and facing a lot of things unexpected

Wiser to let go of worry, dial down overthinking and fears

And slowly fine tune and dial up sensing what the body hears

Thus, a breathing space, a lovely cup of tea or any hot drink

Or even a heavy blanket could slow down all that you overthink

Looking at my wrinkled fins, I know we are not just our racing minds

We inhabit our bodies for sure and soul, even, if one finds

Amidst all the swimming, it helps to feel grounded in the now

And to fully absorb and notice things around you helps somehow

A relief from the cognitive simulations that causes anxiety

And from neverending habitual patterns related to history

Staying mindful, grounded, present or simply being aware is key

Although still in the swimming cycle, a small way to set you free

My thoughts in judgement say- Much easier said than done I hear

Yet another voice says- Don't give in, Let's try it, why fear?

Pausing every now and then, Like anything might be a new habit

Slowly building up from 30 sec to a minute then to 20 might do it

To feel present, truly connecting with a loved one might help

And hugging a friend, stroking a pet and feeling nature- Kelp

Upping activity helps- Breaking a sweat and moving too

And simply engaging in having fun, be curious about you

Swimming in the common ocean, we all have fears and hopes

Yet as individuals, we have unique preferences for soaps

As I swim into another whirlpool, I know not to feel isolated

No matter what, we are beautifully unique and intricately connected

#16 Impatience to Forgiveness

I find myself back between the walls of the Well

Since I cannot see it whole, it seems like a shell

When I swim right to the middle, it all seems vast

I could be in the Ocean, swimming forever to last

Yet a soft voice inside me says I cannot give up

Through another window I go, albeit with an empty cup

I feel free, surfing the tides of the Pacific Ocean

Free, as I've boxed up all past hurts and commotion

I was in a bad place, I'm now with a wife and son

Not a single thing or person will spoil my fun

My wife is kind and loving, I am indeed blessed

It is because of her, I visit family, though unimpressed

I have many unresolved feelings and they trigger those

I'd rather focus on my present and remain in repose

When I last let them in, we saw my little sister react

We exchanged words that we'd rather retract

She's been very sick since and quick to apologise

Though feelings and words I merely recognise

I sometimes feel angry, why did she not know?

She pushed my bottled up emotions to overflow

Yet I can sense her sadness on the other side

Unable to rest, with many feelings on high tide

She'd say, she learnt "Not to reason with a mum, new

Especially if you're soon to be one yourself too"

My wife and sister had an unfortunate dispute

I felt compelled to take sides, a hasty shoot

As I ponder swimming towards the Ocean, I feel good

I can clearly gauge what I previously misunderstood

Looking inwards, I forgot to forgive myself, importantly

Only I, I can let go of what I've been holding onto tightly

#15 Irritation to Self-Care

Finding myself back against the blue brick wall

That well in the ocean, standing majestic and tall

This time, I start from the far left, with a deep sigh

Looking at all those windows that stack up high

I'm a school girl, I am in tears in the shower

I feel no joy, no love, no sense of power

I cannot study, eat, or sleep, I hardly speak

I miss things from the past, can't tweak

I never felt understood, now or then

I have failed to express it all using a pen

Exploring what I truly missed from the past

It was good clothes, food and company that last

Week by week, I made little changes indeed

I called my friends abroad, expressing my need

My heart was growing a bit more open

I was able to talk more to men and women

I bought a few things to cheer myself up

I changed my hair and bought makeup

I finally recognised myself with a smile

My eating and sleeping got better by a mile

I fell out with a good friend as they were controlling

It made sense later although it hurt in the beginning

Yet I had to deal with something else still

My dad, shocked with recent changes in bill

I don't think he understands that finally I feel

Or else he would not be so intent to steal

The joy, the love and the sense of power

That I finally feel when singing in the shower

Surely he has been through his set of windows?

And dealt with life's ways, in columns and rows

#14 Frustration to Compassion

A puddle of tears is what I find myself in

Alas, stuck like a fish on land, without any fin

I was feeling quite the opposite, just a few days ago,

How could I be so dismayed now, is it my ego?

Beneath contempt is sometimes worse than pain

Feeling disrespected over and over yet again

How are things fair when one overdoes it?

Yet the other fools around and behaves illicit

A third person of a curious nature may ponder

"Can she not see in herself, the world of wonder?

What she does arises of her own good nature

What he doesn't fulfil is his remit, not her torture

Each man to himself, regarding accountability

His feelings, thoughts and action, his responsibility

The dilemma is such that her good nature keeps her

Despite his tomfoolery, when she deserves better

Yet easy to say when it happens to someone else

And difficult to follow when you're tidying the fells

It seems like he's eating and having the cake

And she's left high and dry, to scrape and rake

Perhaps he is suffering due to reasons beyond

Yet it's his role to unpick for clarity in the murky pond

He must surely be having fun in the meanwhile

This is no way for her to live, somehow docile

Whether she leaves him or not is up to none

She could gather courage to love herself and have fun"

All this does makes a whole lot of sense to me

My situation doesn't change yet I feel a tad free

Just then I feel the heavens open and rain generate

I'm back in water, perhaps my fin will regenerate?

#13 Pessimism to Grieving

Being back at the Well feels utterly futile

I should be somewhere else worthwhile

I swim through a darker window this time

Just because, no rhythm, no rhyme

I am in sadness, in tears, I am bereaved

Although for my friend in pain, she's relieved

Bless her soul, may she rest in peace

All my love for her will never cease

If I may, I do feel troubled with a few things

What she did in the past sometimes stings

Am I a bad person to think and feel this way?

I know at some level, she led me astray

I broke up with my partner around then

Where was he, I needed him when

The others must have known what he did

It hurts they decided to keep it all hid

I walk down the corridor holding my chest

My heartbeat is racing, I smoke to rest

Until I chance met an old friend in the market

His kind words and tactics made it clear cut

Objectivity and distance are key he said

Replaying these scenes on TV in my head

I saw my character facing tragedies galore

I see why others didn't dare stress me more

They tried to protect me, yet I preferred to know

That my ex partner had no good will to show

My friend might have been wrong but tried

And it is okay for me to love her despite

Love for me is a warm blanket against fears

I miss her, can't help but shed more tears

#12 Boredom and Safety

As I panic, trying to swim up, the whirlpool thrashes me down

I repeat this process like a trapped bee, Oh don't frown

What would you do, just sit, watch and pass a comment?

I have no time for such lazy and effortless lament

I catch myself feeling heavy, making me want to withdraw

I find myself giving in, looking at and relaxing my paw

No doubt, I sink, I drown right to the bottom of the bed

Looking up at the murky waters resonates with content in my head

As all the macro- and micro-particles settle down with me

I feel deeply bored instead of ecstatically free

I have always felt this way in gatherings, small or big

Amidst the noise of chattering, whatever the topic

I am reserved from sharing my personal opinion

Be it politics or judging someone peeling their onion

Perhaps I don't want to commit to either side

You would say I may be kind to do so, beside

The truth remains, I don't engage and self-isolate

My window to share passes by me before I perforate

Perhaps I don't have deep knowledge in anything

Yet you would say does anyone who says a thing

Why do I deflect from an opportunity to be a part?

And insist on being a passenger on life's cart

All I am most interested in, is the subject of "moi"

To tend to my inner child versus any other blah blah

I know the child in me was punished, not loved

Perhaps that explains why my conversations are safely coved

Previously, I have not received kindness and nurture

And quite frankly, I'm past the age to entertain any torture

Hence I may be bored, but I keep safe right here

Be it at the bottom of the well in the certainty of no fear

#11 Positivity despite Addiction

I wake up, looking for a drink, not the one you think

I need alcohol, to make me rise and sink

I stay sober for a month or two in a stretch

Until the beast grabs me for an off-guard fetch

"One's too many, thousand's not enough"

I drink until I feel no discomfort, no cough

I don't think I can ever be fully sober again

I started drinking too early, I was in pain

It made me look cool, I gained friends and fans

I used to write music, travel and pose tans

I then became a workaholic and a partner

I ran into many unseen problems, all a blur

I look around and see my dysfunctional family

I can see it's them, not me, pleased I was able to flee

Did they leave me though, I bet I can still hear them

There are deep in my psyche, still banging a drum

I suppose at some point I must stop blaming

Take responsible for my addiction, to start naming

I hear I have these neural streams in my mind

I can substitute but addictive things, it will find

If so, I dedicate myself to building robust

I will start from myself, without going bust

Then I will build whoever wants to improve

I will employ logic, emotions and stories to move

For what is the meaning of life without

Finding a meaning in life whilst you're about

I am damned sure drinking from dawn to dusk

Ain't why my genes survived the fittest of the tusk

As I build and build, I will stop for a break

And every now and then, I'll enjoy that cake

#10 Content despite Failure

I swim like Night Shimmer Glittering in the Light of Day

Often sighing in frustration that no one can see or pray

Positivity assures me- All you need is to wait for your turn

For the day to end and the night to burn

And then maybe you can shine in your own light

Even Glitter, glimmer or shimmer bright

Often I feel like night shimmer and can relate

Those who are gifted do not seem to wait

They glitter spontaneously in the light of the day

And everything in life seems to fall their way

As night shimmer, I have often wondered and felt flawed

But now know time is too precious to be wastefully flowed

So instead I stop doubting and glitter in any way I can

In the absence of a stage, I believe I know my plan

And when and if my turn shall be

I won't show up desolate but free

This belief, gives me peace it might be though

Disbelief- A dream of the night glittering at low

in the light of the day just like you

Still I can relate and see your view

I am pleased to know I have started to meditate

Whilst swimming, I can connect to a selfless me, early or late

My precious time bubble has indeed burst, it is not fate

I will probably need to act now, not dwell on past hate

And you know what, Perhaps any glitter at night, day or dusk

Might inspire a song to a bird or a tree, wheat or husk

Why is it that I must act for an audience

Can I sometimes simply be in the ambience?

Like this beautiful almost floating coral I can see

Was it randomly placed here, or chosen thee

#9 Belief amidst Self-Doubt

This time it feels like there is no end to this cycle

I try a new window I live the lives of Sam and Michael

No matter how hard I try, I suffer and hurt

Despite solutions I bring to the random issues that skirt

I don't want to swim, I'll just lay on the bottom

I don't want to move, to yet again fail to rotten

I feel numb at first, stuck, unable to breathe with ease

Then I realise, I'm deeply disappointed, on my knees

Further down, I'm really sad feeling heavy

All the burdens and expectations on my heart, levy

I'm tired, I'm low on resources, yet I'm enough

I don't need to pretend to be him or her, up to snuff

That releases a bit of tension, opening up space

Letting my heart settle down to its natural pace

I've liked to know, to plan, to trouble-shoot and charge

Facing so many uncertainties has hijacked me at large

Who am I in this process? Have I paused to care?

Or am I running errands for others, without a minute to spare

Who's life am I living? What has it become?

It looks great on paper, I can prove it's awesome

In the fear of breaking peace, I'm not me

To fit roles and duties I have, I'm not free

Feeling this discomfort makes me wonder

Will I ever be certain if my heart will grow fonder?

It's when I let go of that tunnel vision to solve

I notice there is an area of the well dissolved

I swim up close to this darker, deeper spot

Passing through the crevices, bothered and hot

Yet with some faith that it will all be okay

To realise I'm finally out of the well, at the ocean bay

#8 Hope and Anxiety

Out of the well, I started my CBT therapy sessions with Hayden

I checked my emails and found his latest email he'd done

It's title was "Blueprinting for the future" and recaps a wrap

Reading it, I recall my problem was a post-Cancer frappe

I was starting the 4th harsh treatment, felt like non stop swimming

The period after that long year felt like me finally emerging

I felt tight in my chest, short of breath and overall numb

The ongoing treatment of hormone suppression made me feel dumb

I worried about what had happened, the treatments and where I was

I worried about the future, if there was one without a fuss

I felt on top of it all, an insurmountable pressure to return to work

I was shaking, sweating and knew my scientific hub would lurk

Hayden asked me if I was getting support and empathy

Including myself, my closest circles are a bit distant from sympathy

We've known to show up, work hard, some chill more than the others

Facing challenges, shrugging shoulders worked the figures

With CBT, I delved deeper and found some learnings, very helpful

Especially the worry diary and thinking styles that were unhelpful

The formulation blew my mind, I rescripted my core belief to new

Moreover it joined the dots between worrying and feeling blue

I could then see anxiety and depression playing on a seesaw

Assertive skills for boundaries and self-compassion became my law

The lawyer and prosecutor exercise examined the evidence

For my claim "I won't achieve at work, I'll suffer on the fence"

The cost and benefit way of problem solving sounded witty

I had overlooked this method in general, relying heavily on creativity

But at the time, I had no real access to my creativity nor intuition

Let's be honest, probably, it felt safer to completely shun

Attention focus was a clever tool to deal with something hard

I had heard of it before, yet never used it to yard

#7 Optimism versus Control

Being in nature, seeing Leaves on the stream floating away

I wondered Where these were going, no one way

Yet as humans we struggle, push and pull

We try to control and manage things in full

How can we control waves we couldn't have seen coming

To learn how to surf would be a wiser undergoing

Then we start to believe in our own ability

No matter what, we don't doubt our capability

What surfing means to one individual may

Be unique to them as they themselves say

Yet we are fundamentally all the same

In need of food, water, shelter, love and no shame

Each of us have these rich tapestries

Of memories, experiences and perception pastries

Being aware is the first step to entering

And tapping into this most exciting calling

It brings to life otherwise mundane details

As if a black and white art sans colours, curtails

Nothing judgemental about living one way or the other

As long as one knows, evaluates and chooses this brother

Because to live sleepwalking would be unfortunate

Like a rose withering away as weed and termed fate

Karma in fact is not predetermined destiny as such

It means action, akin to sow as you reap much

So next time you think anything, even coffee drives you

Pause, you drive you and made a decision for you

Optimism is a choice and a path and you are in charge

When you are ready that is, despite the barge

I am no longer swimming incessantly, I want to walk

Perhaps what helped most was being authentic to freely talk

#6 Enthusiasm in Fear

As I started walking with optimism, I looked up into the skies

In awe and inspiration, skipping, following the beautiful bird flies

I looked at my notes again- Achievement Closeness Enjoyment, it said

Aiming for one was good apparently, not everything like I was fed

In the past, at each point, I'd strive to achieve, connect and enjoy

Yet we all know deep down that constantly achieving could be killjoy

Until we get to the destination, which by the way, has no guarantee

"Yet the journey is as important or to connect or simply enjoy brie"

What? Enjoying simply meant relaxing and that was okay?

I didn't need to feel guilty when I would eat, love and pray!?

Better even, the concept of "What would the wise woman say?"

Made me dig deeper and create this self-compassionate ray

I was then able to see very clearly in that light

Self-criticism and self-judgement made me fight or flight

So returning to this topic of an insurmountable pressure I felt

And the uncertainty of cancer and its recurrence belt

The pressure was self-built within, as I self-expected a lot

And needing to know something outside my control was caught

Long before I met A, who re-inspired me to write poetry again

I had written a short poem for Hayden for helping me with my pain

"When the tides were high, moods were low

Not a soul to truly decode my sigh and words of woe

You held the space to hear me out

Nudged to convince me- I'm not a trout

I know you'll say, I'll rise and shine

I probably will or not^ but I'll miss you fine

(^not- because my new rule for living says

"do what I can" versus "be perfect, as it pays"

And I started doing what I could- feeding the homeless over 2 years

Raising a community feel, a zest for life, instead of feeding my fears

#5 Happiness in Spontaneity

As I started walking and skipping, rigidity broke free

I wanted to dance for myself like no one can see

I started looking for a fun, group dance class here

Finding something trendy around me would be rare

Perhaps Salsa or Bhangra would be loud, lively and fun

Not much chance of such options in the nearby town, Hun

Instead I found a cultural dance class for all

Parents of children could join with them, short and tall

It was none other than the classical dance

Of Indian Bharatnatyam, it demanded a stance

This possibility transported me back to when I was 10

And saw S perform Bharatnatyam at school then

I was fascinated and wanted to learn

I cannot recall if I even said so to anyone in turn

Here, many years later, I could pick up that dream

Would it benefit Huni, maybe, that's another stream

I suppose I was showing up, this was exercise

It helped me recover, claim a sleeping dream and rise

Within weeks, we were working on a duet

I felt incompetent and like an undeserving suet

My dance buddy was both kind and consistent

She helped me practise and keep it persistent

We even danced at a local festival on stage

So did Huni with her group, filling our memory page

I was clueless that the same evening, on the main podium

Apache Indian and Punjabi MC shook the rhodium

I was startled when I read that a few days later

Musical legends I listened to in the past performed right there

In my own world, a lot had been again shaken

It helped despite visiting the A&E with symptoms mistaken

#4 Empowerment and Faith

You'd think walking and skipping, I'd live happily ever after

If only life stopped testing us, awarding more ailments amidst BAFTAs

They say emotions are powerful and contagious and yes they are

That's how I felt after chance meeting my positive friend, Jen, not far

I saw her a couple of times doing the school run

Initiated a chat and learnt she cares about health and fun

It was very easy to befriend her

In fact seeing her made my days brighter

She then opened up about a wellbeing community

Her architecture career, kids, love for travel and sustainability

Like myself, she cared for the planet, fitness and health

Having gone through setbacks, I knew good health was wealth

I got more curious about these products she used

I tried the product samples, her eagerness, I could not refuse

This mascara, was top 10 in the Wall Street Chart

It helped my eyelashes grow, I hit the dart

I loved the anti-redness compact powder too

I am not fond of the effect on my face of the extra red hue

The protein tasted good and helped me manage my weight

Post-treatment I lost 10 kilos, caring for exercise and what I ate

The gut health product helped me balance my microbiome

After many prescribed medications concocted in the fume

As a scientist, I stayed analytical at first, hesitant to join

Under the surface, I felt underlying fears, yet to coin

I joined this free online club, offering wellbeing and inspiring stories

Hearing from Rach and others beat so many of my worries

Having the chance to witness my first live motivational

Felt surreal, having so much respect for this path creational

I felt eager and empowered and looking forwards to life

More in the flow, at ease and accepting, putting behind strife

#3 Love and Self-Love

I am ashore again laying blissfully on the sands

Watching the dance between the tides and the lands

I am full of love, I feel loved, I doubt no more

If I were at the bottom of the sea or on the land ashore

I know I am enough, when I win and overperform

Or when I fail and feel despondent to underperform

The core of me has been seen and I feel truly me

That inevitably impacts my close relationships to be

When love is in the air, I am in the flow, no rigid demands

In appreciation and forgiveness, hardly any reprimand

Letting go of expectations, and able to live in the now

Making it all so wonderful and easy amidst the plough

Sometimes we happily sit when we truly want to fly

As we feel love for our loved ones who may be shy

Doesn't help to have been fed fairy tales of knight in shining armour

When all we truly need is safety, engagement and soothing to feel calmer

Genuine love allows space to fly and sit still

There is no set formula to fit the bill!

Love understands that people continuously evolve

We're not solid planets that routinely revolve

Yet it has patience and compassion to withstand

Truly be there, have fun and totally understand

The biggest learning yet was love is never a fix

Hard to fathom, if unhappy and devoid of felix

To truly love, I knew to turn inwards

And invite self-love to share onwards

Love has many names, beyond puppy and wren

Spouse, parents, siblings, gran, uncles, aunts and children

#2 Gratitude and Joy

I'm not in the well, how surreal as I look from above and into it

Seeing a continuous diaspora of wonderful ripples, they're perfect- innit!?

I pluck and offer this mysterious well a couple of clovers and blues

Holding my awareness and expectations gently, as the text imbues

I catch my automatic thought saying "You'll make no impact"

Then checked in with my feeling: "disbelief", now that's a fine tact

I sensed a pleasant *Vedana* tone, when I heard a soft plop

Turning towards my direct sensations freed me from a flop

Better still, I was mesmerised by those perfect diffractions

When my flowers appeared clearing my mind off all distractions

I ticked off mindfulness and breathing space exercises off my list

Gratitude was next and five things could only describe the gist

Of how grateful I've been this weekend, firstly to my hubby

For happily willing to look after our kids and watch Teletubby

Then, SR, for his teachings on the Worldly Winds and *Hri*

Hri, positive self-shame with resolution, from sorry *Hri* to *Shri*

Kshyama, forgiveness truly restoring undistorted *mata*, logic

Together, gathering *kshyamata*, enabled capacity and magic

Moreover, when *hri*, forgiveness and *daya*, kindness get integrated

Hridaya, heart openly pours into art, fearless of getting berated

Grateful to AC, mother compassion personified

And many friends and Sangha members, lovely and dignified

Finally to return to Buddha, mind's highest potential

Calm and steady in sunshine and rains torrential

Luckily, I have good access to *mudita* and *karuna* despite enmity

I'd like to deepen *metta* for myself and *upekkha*, equanimity

I offer this writing as a gift for giving and for considering

With that I've completed my exercise for Chapter three

Yayy, no more hands on my face and sulking on my knee

I feel energetic, having found an inspiration to break free

#1 Freedom and Nature

My heart sings a song

Or are the birds furlong?

The skies are sunset pink

With a tinge of coral wink

I'm alone yet not alone

Surrounded in nature, no phone

Content in connections I share

Grateful for "me time" to spare

There is peaceful stillness within

The reasons for which are hard to pin

Is it nature, the stupa or the pond?

Is it the shrine or a spiritual bond?

I'm where I'm supposed to be

My heart is cautious, yet brave to glee

I see the green grasses swish

I bet I could guarantee a wish

Yet I choose higher values

Service, Abundance, Peace, Hues

When these are in store

Bad luck or good, wealth is galore

This is when I thrive

Simple things, alive

I'm grateful to my partner because

We leapt in, tried and grew for a cause

I'm grateful to my parents and siblings as

They gave their best whatever has

I forgive those and myself

Free to action, off that shelf

I may not be able to literally fly

My spirits are free soaring up in the sky

Closing Remarks

I hope this book offers you inspiration. For further inspiration, please
consider reading "The Guest House" by Rumi.

If you feel inspired to write, and/or share any feedback, please leave me a
review. I look forward to hearing from you!

Much Love, O.K. x